Robert Rose's
Favorite
SNACKS·SALADS & APPETIZERS

Robert
ROSE

ROBERT ROSE'S FAVORITE SNACKS • SALADS AND APPETIZERS

Copyright © 1998 Robert Rose Inc.

Canadian Cataloguing in Publication Data

Main entry under title:

Robert Rose's favorite snacks, salads & appetizers

Includes index.

ISBN 1-896503-51-9

1. Snack foods. 2. Salads. 3. Appetizers I. Title: Snacks, salads & appetizers.

TX740.R62 1998   641.8'12   C98-930499-X

DESIGN AND PAGE COMPOSITION: MATTHEWS COMMUNICATIONS DESIGN
PHOTOGRAPHY: MARK T. SHAPIRO

Cover photo: AVOCADO TOMATO SALSA, PAGE 37

Distributed in the U.S. by: Distributed in Canada by:
Firefly Books (U.S.) Inc.   Stoddart Publishing Co. Ltd.
P.O. Box 1338   34 Lesmill Road
Ellicott Station   North York, Ontario
Buffalo, NY   14205   M3B 2T6

ORDER LINES
Tel: (416) 499-8412
Fax: (416) 499-8313

ORDER LINES
Tel: (416) 445-3333
Fax: (416) 445-5967

Published by: Robert Rose Inc. • 156 Duncan Mill Road, Suite 12
Toronto, Ontario, Canada M3B 2N2 Tel: (416) 449-3535

Printed in Canada   1234567 BP 01 00 99 98

About this book

At Robert Rose, we're committed to finding imaginative and exciting ways to provide our readers with cookbooks that offer great recipes — and exceptional value. That's the thinking behind our "Robert Rose's Favorite" series.

Here we've selected over 55 favorite recipes from a number of our bestselling full-sized cookbooks: Byron Ayanoglu's *New Vegetarian Gourmet* and *Simply Mediterranean Cooking*; Johanna Burkhard's *Comfort Food Cookbook*; Andrew Chase's *Asian Bistro Cookbook*; *New World Noodles* and *New World Chinese Cooking*, by Bill Jones and Stephen Wong; and Rose Reisman's *Light Cooking, Light Pasta, Enlightened Home Cooking* and *Light Vegetarian Cooking*. As well, we've included recipes from our own *Robert Rose's Classic Pasta*.

We believe that it all adds up to great value for anyone who loves snacks, salads and appetizers.

Want to find out more about the sources of our recipes? See pages 94 and 95 for details.

Contents

Appetizers

Snacks

Salads

Appetizers

Smoked Salmon Mousse

Makes 3 cups (750 mL)

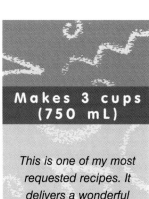

This is one of my most requested recipes. It delivers a wonderful smoked salmon flavor, but uses relatively little of that costly ingredient. My secret? I work magic with canned salmon, which keeps the cost reasonable so I can serve this appetizer more often.

TIP

I prefer to use canned sockeye salmon (instead of the pink variety) for its superior color and flavor.

The mousse can be prepared up to 4 days ahead for easy entertaining.

To get more juice out of a lemon, roll on counter top or microwave at High for 20 seconds before squeezing.

FROM
THE COMFORT FOOD COOKBOOK BY JOHANNA BURKHARD

1/3 cup	dry white wine *or* water	75 mL
1	pkg (1/4 oz [7 g]) unflavored gelatin	1
1	can (7 1/2 oz [213 g]) sockeye salmon, drained, skin removed	1
1 cup	sour cream	250 mL
1 tbsp	fresh lemon juice	15 mL
1/2 tsp	grated lemon rind	2 mL
1/4 tsp	salt	1 mL
	Hot pepper sauce, to taste	
4 oz	smoked salmon, finely chopped	125 g
2 tbsp	minced green onions	25 mL
2 tbsp	finely chopped fresh dill	25 mL
1/2 cup	whipping (35%) cream, whipped	125 mL
	Dill sprigs and lemon zest for garnish	

1. Place wine in a small bowl; sprinkle gelatin over. Let stand 5 minutes to soften. Microwave at Medium for 1 minute or until dissolved.

2. In a food processor, combine canned salmon, sour cream, lemon juice and rind, salt and hot pepper sauce; process until smooth. Add gelatin mixture; process until combined.

3. Transfer mixture to a bowl. Stir in smoked salmon, onions and dill; fold in whipped cream.

4. Spoon mixture into serving dish. Cover loosely with plastic wrap (it should not touch surface of the mousse); refrigerate for 4 hours or overnight. Garnish top with dill sprigs and lemon zest; serve with melba toast or pumpernickel rounds.

Makes 2 1/2 cups (625 mL)

Here's a modern spin to an old standby, chicken liver spread. Even if you're not a big fan of liver, you'll be instantly won over when you try this lightly sweetened pâté with currants and Port. Serve with warm toasted baguette slices.

TIP

Make the pâté up to 3 days ahead. Cover surface with plastic wrap and refrigerate. Or pack into containers and freeze for up to 1 month.

•

Like freshly ground pepper, the taste of freshly grated nutmeg is so much better than the pre-ground variety. Whole nutmeg can be found in the spice section of your supermarket or bulk food store. Look for inexpensive nutmeg graters in kitchenware shops.

FROM
THE COMFORT FOOD COOKBOOK BY JOHANNA BURKHARD

Party Pâté

3 tbsp	dried currants	45 mL
3 tbsp	ruby Port	45 mL
1 lb	chicken livers	500 g
2 tbsp	butter	25 mL
1	medium onion, finely chopped	1
1 cup	peeled, chopped apples	250 mL
3/4 tsp	salt	4 mL
1/2 tsp	rubbed sage	2 mL
1/2 tsp	pepper	2 mL
1/4 tsp	nutmeg	1 mL
1/3 cup	butter, cut into small cubes	75 mL

1. In a small glass dish, combine currants and Port; microwave at High for 1 minute until plump. Set aside.

2. Trim chicken livers and cut into quarters. Place in a large nonstick skillet with 1/2 cup (125 mL) water; bring to a boil over medium heat, stirring often, for 5 minutes or until no longer pink. Drain in sieve; transfer to bowl of food processor.

3. Rinse and dry skillet; add 2 tbsp (25 mL) of the butter and melt over medium heat. Add onion, apples, salt, sage, pepper and nutmeg; cook, stirring often, for 5 minutes or until softened.

4. Add onion-apple mixture to liver in bowl of food processor; purée until very smooth. Let cool slightly. Add butter cubes to liver mixture and purée until creamy. Add reserved currants and Port; pulse, using on-off turns, until just combined.

5. Spoon into a serving bowl. Cover surface with plastic wrap and refrigerate until firm, about 4 hours or overnight.

Serves 4

Asparagus Wrapped with Ricotta Cheese and Ham

PREHEAT OVEN TO 400° F (200° C)
BAKING SHEET SPRAYED WITH VEGETABLE SPRAY

12	medium asparagus, trimmed	12
4 oz	ricotta cheese	125 g
1/4 tsp	crushed garlic	1 mL
1 tbsp	finely chopped green onion or chives	15 mL
	Salt and pepper	
4	thin slices cooked ham (about 4 oz [125 g])	4

1. Steam or microwave asparagus just until tender-crisp; drain and let cool. Set aside.

2. In a small bowl, combine cheese, garlic, onion, and salt and pepper to taste; mix well.

3. Spread evenly over each slice of ham. Top each with 3 asparagus and roll up. Place on baking sheet and bake for 3 to 4 minutes or until hot.

Serves 6 to 8

Oriental Egg Rolls with Almond Sauce

PREHEAT OVEN TO 425° F (220°C)
BAKING SHEET SPRAYED WITH VEGETABLE SPRAY

TIP

If you're using a store-bought pesto sauce, the calories and fat will be higher.

•

If in a hurry, you don't need to chill the tortilla before cutting. Just use a sharp knife.

•

If tortillas are very small, increase the number to 8.

•

Try 4 oz (125 g) roasted sweet peppers in a jar to replace fresh pepper. Use those which are packed in water.

MAKE AHEAD

Prepare up to a day ahead, keeping tightly wrapped in refrigerator. Preheat broiler

FROM
ROSE REISMAN'S ENLIGHTENED HOME COOKING

Sauce

2 tbsp	finely chopped almonds	25 mL
4 tsp	soya sauce	20 mL
1 tbsp	sesame oil	15 mL
1 tbsp	honey	15 mL
2 tbsp	chicken stock *or* water	25 mL
1 tbsp	rice wine vinegar	15 mL
1 tsp	minced garlic	5 mL
1 tsp	minced ginger root	5 mL

Filling

3/4 cup	finely chopped red peppers	175 mL
3/4 cup	finely chopped snow peas	175 mL
1/2 cup	finely chopped green onions (about 4 medium)	125 mL
1 1/4 cups	bean sprouts	300 mL
3/4 cup	finely chopped crab legs or surimi (imitation crab)	175 mL
1/4 cup	chopped fresh coriander *or* parsley	50 mL
10	large egg roll wrappers	10

1. In food processor or in a bowl, combine almonds, soya sauce, sesame oil, honey, chicken stock, vinegar, garlic and ginger. Process or mix until well combined. Set aside.

2. In a large nonstick skillet sprayed with vegetable spray, cook the red peppers, snow peas and green onions over medium-high heat for 4 minutes or until tender-crisp. Add bean sprouts, crab, and 2 tbsp (25 mL) of the sauce; cook, stirring, for 2 more minutes. Remove from heat and stir in coriander.

3. Keeping rest of wrappers covered with a cloth to prevent drying out, put 1 wrapper on work surface with a corner pointing towards you. Put 1/4 cup (50 mL) of the filling in the center. Fold the lower corner up over the filling, fold the two side corners in over the filling and roll the bundle away from you. Place on prepared pan and repeat until all wrappers are filled. Bake for 12 to 14 minutes until slightly browned, turning the egg rolls at the halfway point. Serve with dipping sauce.

TIP

If you're using a store-bought pesto sauce, the calories and fat will probably be higher.

•

If in a hurry, you don't need to chill the tortilla before cutting. Just use a sharp knife.

•

If tortillas are very small, increase the number to 8.

•

Try 4 oz (125 g) of roasted sweet peppers in a jar to replace fresh pepper. Use those which are packed in water.

MAKE AHEAD

Prepare up to a day ahead, keeping tightly wrapped in refrigerator. Preheat broiler

FROM
ROSE REISMAN'S ENLIGHTENED HOME COOKING

Pesto and Red Pepper Tortilla Bites

3 tbsp	pesto sauce (store-bought or homemade)	45 mL
3 oz	goat cheese	75 g
1/4 cup	5% ricotta cheese	50 mL
1	large red pepper	1
3	10-inch (25 cm) flour tortillas	3
	or	
6	6-inch (15 cm) flour tortillas	6

1. In a bowl or food processor, combine pesto, goat cheese and ricotta; mix until well combined.

2. Roast pepper under the broiler for 15 to 20 minutes, turning several times until charred on all sides; place in a bowl covered tightly with plastic wrap; let stand until cool enough to handle. Remove skin, stem and seeds; cut roasted pepper into thin strips.

3. If using larger tortillas, spread 1/4 cup (50 mL) filling on each tortilla; if using smaller tortillas, spread 2 tbsp (25 mL) on each tortilla. Spread filling to edges of tortillas, scatter red pepper strips on top, and roll tightly. Chill, wrapped in plastic wrap, for an hour. Cut into 1-inch (2.5 cm) pieces and serve.

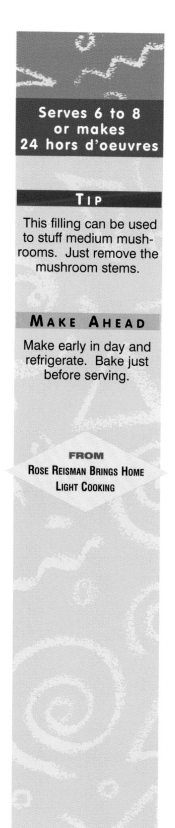

Serves 6 to 8
or makes
24 hors d'oeuvres

TIP

This filling can be used to stuff medium mushrooms. Just remove the mushroom stems.

MAKE AHEAD

Make early in day and refrigerate. Bake just before serving.

FROM
ROSE REISMAN BRINGS HOME LIGHT COOKING

Warm Cherry Tomatoes Stuffed with Garlic and Cheese

PREHEAT OVEN TO 400° F (200° C)

24	cherry tomatoes	24
1/2 cup	dry bread crumbs	125 mL
2 tbsp	chopped green onions	25 mL
1/2 tsp	chopped garlic	2 mL
2 tbsp	chopped fresh parsley	25 mL
1 tbsp	margarine, melted	15 mL
1/3 cup	shredded mozzarella cheese	75 mL
1 tbsp	grated Parmesan cheese	15 mL

1. Cut slice from top of each tomato; carefully scoop out seeds and most of the pulp.

2. In bowl, combine bread crumbs, onion, garlic, parsley, margarine and mozzarella until well mixed.

3. Spoon into tomatoes; sprinkle with Parmesan. Place on baking sheet and bake for approximately 10 minutes or until stuffing is golden.

Fresh Vegetable Spring Rolls with Filipino Garlic Sauce

Serves 6

Most Southeast Asian countries have a version of fresh spring rolls. Filipinos have adapted the original Fukien unfried spring rolls (lun bia) to one of their national dishes, fresh lumpia. They are usually made from fresh heart of palm, a delicacy unfortunately unavailable here. The wrappers are generally made of wheat flour, starch and egg, and are steamed and cooled before use. Vietnamese are famous for a wide range of uncooked spring rolls wrapped in "rice paper" — thin, round sheets of cooked glutinous rice that merely have to be soaked in warm water and rolled up around a filling. Here we have combined both traditions.

Vary the amounts of the vegetables or change them according to personal taste and what is available.

FROM
THE ASIAN BISTRO COOKBOOK BY ANDREW CHASE

Garlic Sauce

1 tbsp	vegetable oil	15 mL
2 tbsp	minced garlic	25 mL
1 cup	vegetable stock *or* chicken stock	250 mL
1/2 cup	granulated sugar	125 mL
4 tsp	soya sauce	20 mL
1/4 tsp	black pepper	1 mL
2 1/2 tbsp	rice vinegar *or* 3 tbsp (45 mL) lime juice	35 mL
2 1/2 tsp	cornstarch mixed with 1 tbsp (15 mL) water	12 mL

Spring Rolls

Half	package (2 oz [50 g]) bean threads (optional)	Half
3 oz	string beans	75 g
3 oz	pea pods (snow peas)	75 g
3 oz	bean sprouts	75 g
2 oz	carrot julienne	50 g
3 oz	jicama julienne	75 g
1 oz	red bell pepper julienne	25 g
12	sheets "rice paper" wrappers	12
6	leaf lettuce leaves, cut in half	6
1/4 cup	loosely packed Thai basil leaves (optional)	50 mL

1. In a saucepan heat oil over low heat; cook garlic 2 minutes without browning. Stir in stock, sugar, soya sauce and pepper; increase heat to simmer and cook 2 minutes. Stir in vinegar; cook 1 minute. Stir in cornstarch mixture; cook 30 seconds or until thickened. Transfer to a serving bowl; cool to room temperature.

2. Soak bean threads, if using, in cold water to cover until pliable. Bring a pot with 4 cups (1 L) water to a boil. Blanch the bean threads for 20 seconds, the beans (2 minutes), pea pods (30 seconds), bean sprouts (5 seconds) and carrots (30 seconds), rinsing them all in cold water immediately after blanching to stop further

In North America, jicama is usually thought of as a Mexican ingredient, however it is very common in the Philippines and other Southeast Asian countries, probably as a result of Spanish Asian trade routes through Acapulco and Manila. It is a large round tuber with a thick skin which must be peeled; the slightly sweet crunchy flesh is eaten raw. It's a bit like a cross between an apple and a potato. It is often available at grocery chains, as well as Asian and Central American grocers. Wrapping the spring rolls is an easily acquired skill; just don't be too frustrated if the first batch isn't perfect. Avoid trying to overstuff the wrappers; it is better to have extra filling to make more spring rolls than to struggle with overfilled rolls.

cooking; drain and dry vegetables. Cut beans and pea pods into julienne by cutting lengthwise on a very oblique diagonal. Mix bean threads, beans, pea pods, bean sprouts, carrots, jicama and red pepper.

3. Fill a large bowl with warm water and soak 1 wrapper until soft. Place wrapper on dry cloth, put a lettuce leaf half over it, make a line of 3 or 4 basil leaves and cover with vegetables; roll into a cylinder, tucking in the edges as you roll. Put on a tray and cover with a damp cloth. Repeat with remaining wrappers and filling. Serve with garlic sauce on the side to be spooned over just before eating or, if serving the spring rolls as finger food, to be dunked into.

Variation

- Strips of cold boiled, roasted or Chinese-style barbecued pork make a very nice addition to the spring rolls, as does cold poached shrimp.

TIP

To toast pine nuts, put in nonstick skillet over medium-high heat for 3 minutes, stirring occasionally. Or put them on a baking sheet and toast in a 400° F (200° C) oven for 5 minutes. Whichever method you choose, watch carefully – nuts burn quickly.

•

If basil is not available, use parsley or spinach leaves.

MAKE AHEAD

Prepare early in the day and keep covered and refrigerated.

FROM
ROSE REISMAN'S ENLIGHTENED
HOME COOKING

Creamy Pesto Dip

1 cup	well–packed basil leaves	250 mL
2 tbsp	toasted pine nuts	25 mL
2 tbsp	grated Parmesan cheese	25 mL
2 tbsp	olive oil	25 mL
2 tsp	lemon juice	10 mL
1 tsp	minced garlic	5 mL
1/2 cup	5% ricotta cheese	125 mL
1/4 cup	light sour cream	50 mL

1. Put basil, pine nuts, Parmesan, olive oil, lemon juice and garlic in food processor; process until finely chopped, scraping sides of bowl down once. Add ricotta and sour cream and process until smooth. Serve with pita or tortilla crisps, or fresh vegetables.

FROM
THE NEW VEGETARIAN
GOURMET BY BYRON
AYANOGLU

Serves 4 as an appetizer or 2 as a main course

This is one for those who thought they'd already had every possible combination of pizza toppings. The cheese, which I've marked "optional" (because it works without it) can be anything — mozzarella, cheddar, Parmesan or pecorino Crotonese.

Potato Byzza

PREHEAT OVEN TO **400° F (200° C)**
BAKING SHEET GREASED LIGHTLY WITH OIL

1 lb	potatoes (about 3), unpeeled but well scrubbed	500 g
2 tbsp	olive oil	25 mL
1/4 tsp	salt	2 mL
1/4 tsp	black pepper	2 mL
2	cloves garlic, lightly crushed but not pressed	2
1/2 cup	sliced red onions	125 mL
2	6-inch (15 cm) *naan* or pita breads, *or* pizza crusts	2
1 tbsp	olive oil	15 mL
1	medium tomato, thinly sliced	1
1/2 tsp	dried oregano	2 mL
3	cloves garlic, thinly sliced	3
6	black olives, pitted and chopped	6
2 oz	cheese (optional), shaved	50 g
	Few sprigs fresh dill and/or rosemary, chopped	

1. In a large saucepan cover potatoes with plenty of water and bring to a boil. Cook for 5 minutes, then drain. Cut potatoes into neat 1/4-inch (5 mm) slices. Set aside.

2. In a large frying pan, heat the oil over medium heat. Add salt, pepper and garlic. Sauté 1 to 2 minutes until garlic browns. Remove garlic and discard. Add sliced onions and stir-fry for 1 minute.

3. Push onions to the sides of the pan and, in the middle, place the best-formed of your potato slices to form a single layer. (Reserve any leftover slices for another use.) Reduce heat to minimum and cook about 50 minutes, turning every 10 minutes or so, until potatoes have browned and are soft when pierced. (The onions on the side will be reduced in volume and somewhat charred; discard any that have become too black.)

Recipe continues...

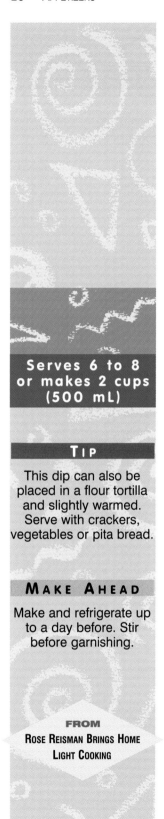

4. Lightly brush both sides of the *naan* breads with the oil and place on a baking sheet. Top with tomato slices, then sprinkle with oregano. Arrange potato slices to cover tomatoes, then top with cooked onions, garlic, olive bits and, if desired, cheese shavings.

5. Bake for 18 to 20 minutes until the bottom of the crusts are crisp. Remove from oven, cut into quarters and garnish with the chopped herb(s). Serve immediately.

Serves 6 to 8 or makes 2 cups (500 mL)

TIP

This dip can also be placed in a flour tortilla and slightly warmed. Serve with crackers, vegetables or pita bread.

MAKE AHEAD

Make and refrigerate up to a day before. Stir before garnishing.

FROM
ROSE REISMAN BRINGS HOME LIGHT COOKING

Spicy Mexican Dip

1 cup	canned refried beans	250 mL
1/3 cup	minced red onion	75 mL
1/3 cup	finely diced sweet red peppers	75 mL
3/4 tsp	crushed garlic	4 mL
2 tsp	chili powder	10 mL
2 tbsp	chopped fresh parsley	25 mL
2 tbsp	2% yogurt	25 mL
2 tsp	lemon juice	10 mL
3 tbsp	crushed bran cereal★	45 mL
	Parsley sprigs	

★ Use a wheat bran breakfast cereal

1. In a bowl combine beans, onion, red pepper, garlic, chili powder, parsley, yogurt, lemon juice and cereal; stir until blended. Place in serving bowl and garnish with parsley sprigs.

Goat Cheese and Spinach Phyllo Triangles

Makes 12

TIP

Phyllo dries out quickly, becoming brittle and hard to handle. Keep phyllo covered with a cloth, exposing only the sheets you're working on.

•

Approximately 4 cups (1 L) fresh spinach can be cooked, drained and the excess liquid squeezed out, in order to get 2/3 cup (150 mL).

MAKE AHEAD

These can be prepared, covered and frozen for up to 2 weeks, or refrigerated for up to one day, covered well. Bake an extra 5 to 10 minutes to heat thoroughly.

FROM
ROSE REISMAN'S ENLIGHTENED
HOME COOKING

PREHEAT OVEN TO 400°F (200°C)
BAKING SHEET SPRAYED WITH VEGETABLE SPRAY

2 tsp	vegetable oil	10 mL
1 1/2 tsp	minced garlic	7 mL
1 cup	finely chopped red onions	250 mL
3/4 cup	finely chopped red peppers	175 mL
2/3 cup	cooked spinach, drained and chopped	150 mL
1/2 cup	5% ricotta cheese	125 mL
3 oz	goat cheese	75 g
3 tbsp	chopped fresh dill (or 1 tsp [5 mL] dried)	45 mL
1 tbsp	grated Parmesan cheese	15 mL
8	sheets phyllo pastry	8
2 tsp	melted margarine or butter	10 mL

1. Heat oil in nonstick skillet over medium heat; add garlic, red onions and red peppers and cook for 5 minutes, or until softened. Remove from heat; stir in spinach, ricotta, goat cheese, dill and Parmesan and mix well.

2. Lay two sheets of phyllo pastry, one on top of the other, on work surface in front of you. Cut lengthwise into three strips. Put 3 tbsp (45 mL) of filling near end of one strip; fold corner up to enclose filling and create a triangle-shaped bundle. Flip bundle repeatedly up and then over until all of phyllo strip has been used. Fill other two strips in same manner; place triangles on prepared baking sheet. Repeat with remaining phyllo sheets.

3. Brush triangles with melted margarine and bake for 10 minutes, or until browned.

FROM
ROSE REISMAN'S LIGHT
VEGETARIAN COOKING

Marinated Greek Mushrooms

Serves 6 to 8

TIP

The longer the mushrooms marinate, the more flavorful they will be.

•

If you can't find small button mushrooms, use larger mushrooms and cut into quarters. To make this a vegan dish, just eliminate the cheese.

MAKE AHEAD

Prepare 1 day in advance. Stir before serving.

1 lb	button mushrooms, cleaned	500 g
1/2 cup	chopped fresh coriander	125 mL
1/2 cup	chopped red onions	125 mL
1/3 cup	sliced black olives	75 mL
1/3 cup	balsamic vinegar	75 mL
2 tbsp	water	25 mL
2 tbsp	olive oil	25 mL
1 tbsp	freshly squeezed lemon juice	15 mL
1 tsp	minced garlic	5 mL
1/2 to 3/4 tsp	chili powder	2 to 4 mL
	or 1/2 tsp (2 mL) minced fresh jalapeno pepper	
1/4 tsp	freshly ground black pepper	1 mL
2 oz	feta cheese, crumbled	50 g

1. In a large bowl, stir together mushrooms, coriander, red onions, olives, vinegar, water, olive oil, lemon juice, garlic, chili powder, pepper and feta.

2. Cover and chill 1 hour or overnight, mixing occasionally.

Caesar Tortilla Pizzas

Serves 4

TIP

I tried this pizza at the Planet Hollywood restaurant in Manhattan; this low-fat version is, I think, even more delicious than the original. Try using pita bread instead of tortillas.

PREHEAT OVEN TO 400° F (200° C)
BAKING SHEET

Sauce

1	egg yolk	1
2 tbsp	grated Parmesan cheese	25 mL
2 tsp	freshly squeezed lemon juice	10 mL
1 tsp	minced garlic	5 mL
1/2 tsp	Dijon mustard	2 mL
2 tbsp	olive oil	25 mL
4	small flour tortillas (6-inch [15 cm])	4
	or 2 large (10-inch [25 cm])	

Toppings

1 cup	diced seeded plum tomatoes	250 mL
3/4 cup	shredded part-skim mozzarella cheese (about 3 oz [75 g])	175 mL
2 tbsp	grated Parmesan cheese	25 mL
1/2 cup	chopped romaine lettuce	125 mL

1. In a small bowl, whisk together egg yolk, 2 tbsp (25 mL) Parmesan cheese, lemon juice, garlic and mustard. Gradually add olive oil, whisking constantly. Put tortillas on baking sheet and divide sauce among tortillas, spreading to the edges.

2. Divide tomatoes, mozzarella and remaining Parmesan among tortillas.

3. Bake 12 to 14 minutes or until cheese melts and tortillas start to brown. Top with lettuce, slice and serve immediately.

Mint Feta Phyllo Nests

Serves 4

In this variation on the previous recipe, we use less expensive feta with a minty twist. The sharp-tasting 3-to-1 ratio of feta to mozzarella can be mellowed by using equal portions (4 oz [125 g]) of each cheese. And if you're using fresh mint (which we heartily recommend), feel free to double the quantity called for in the recipe.

FROM
SIMPLY
MEDITERRANEAN COOKING BY
BYRON AYANOGLU & ALGIS
KEMEZYS

**12-CUP MUFFIN TIN, 8 OF THE CUPS LIGHTLY OILED
PREHEAT OVEN TO 350° F (180° C)**

6 oz	feta cheese, crumbled	175 g
1/2 cup	shredded mozzarella (about 2 oz [50 g])	125 mL
3 tbsp	minced red onions	45 mL
2 tbsp	minced red bell peppers	25 mL
1 tsp	olive oil	5 mL
Pinch	cayenne pepper	Pinch
1/4 cup	chopped fresh mint (or 1 tbsp [15 mL] dried)	50 mL
2	eggs, beaten	2
6	sheets phyllo dough	6
1/4 cup	olive oil	50 mL

1. In a bowl with a fork, mash feta with mozzarella until well crumbled and mixed together. Set aside.

2. In a small nonstick saucepan, combine red onions, red peppers, 1 tsp (5 mL) olive oil and the cayenne pepper. Cook over medium-high heat, stirring, for 4 minutes or until softened but not browned. Remove from heat; stir into cheese mixture. Stir in mint and eggs until well mixed. Cover bowl and refrigerate at least 20 minutes or up to 24 hours.

3. On a dry surface, layer 3 sheets of phyllo on top of one another, lightly brushing with olive oil between layers. Brush top surface with oil. Cut the layered phyllo into quarters. Carefully lift each quarter and gently fit into the middle of an oiled muffin cup, fluting the edges that rise off the cup to resemble a nest. Repeat layer-ing-cutting-nest-building procedure with remaining 3 phyllo sheets to produce a total of 8 nests.

4. Spoon one-eighth of cheese mixture (about 3 tbsp [45 mL]) into each nest.

5. Bake undisturbed for 20 minutes or until phyllo is golden brown and the cheese filling has set. Remove from oven and let rest for 10 minutes. Unmold from the muffin tin (they'll slip off easily). Serve 2 nests per person.

**Serves 6 to 10
as an appetizer**

*We've made these bundles
with ground beef but many
other fillings — such as
prawns with ginger and fish
sauce or salmon with
scallions and garlic —
also come to mind.*

FROM
NEW WORLD NOODLES
**BY BILL JONES & STEPHEN
WONG**

Steamed Beef and Cilantro Bundles

STEAMER, PREFERABLY BAMBOO

Marinade

2 tbsp	oyster sauce	25 mL
1 tbsp	soya sauce	15 mL
1 tsp	freshly ground black pepper	5 mL
1 tsp	cornstarch	5 mL
12 oz	extra-lean ground beef	375 g

Bundles

1 tbsp	vegetable oil	15 mL
1	can (7 oz [175 g]) sliced bamboo shoots, drained and chopped	1
1/2 cup	roasted peanuts	125 mL
1/4 cup	fresh cilantro leaves, finely chopped	50 mL
12	8-inch (20 cm) lengths of green onions (green part only)	12
12	5-inch (12 cm) round sheets Vietnamese rice paper	12

1. In a medium-size bowl combine ingredients for marinade. Add beef, mix well and set aside to marinate for 1 hour.

2. Make the filling: In a nonstick wok or skillet, heat oil over medium-high heat for 30 seconds. Add beef and stir-fry until cooked through, about 3 minutes. Add bamboo shoots and peanuts; stir-fry for 1 minute. Remove from heat and mix in cilantro leaves. Allow to cool.

3. In a large pot of boiling water, blanch green onions until just wilted, about 15 to 20 seconds. Remove and plunge into a bowl of ice water. Drain and set aside.

4. Half-fill a large heatproof bowl or pot with boiling water. Using tongs or chopsticks, immerse a sheet of rice paper in water until it's soft and pliable, about 2 or 3 seconds. Remove sheet, pat dry with a paper towel and lay the sheet on a flat, dry surface. Place 1 heaping tablespoon (15-20 mL) of filling in the center, then gather up the edges of the wrap and tie into a bundle with one of the blanched green onions. Repeat

procedure with the remaining ingredients. Bundles can be made a few hours ahead and kept in the refrigerator, covered with a damp towel.

5. Just before serving, place bundles in a preheated, lightly oiled steamer and steam for 2 minutes or until heated through. Serve immediately with Nuoc Cham (see recipe, following), chili oil or Tabasco sauce as an accompaniment.

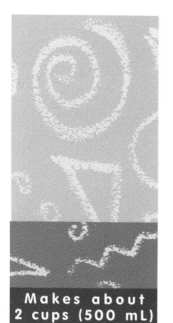

**Makes about
2 cups (500 mL)**

This all-purpose dipping sauce can be found in most Vietnamese kitchens. It makes a wonderful dressing for noodles and vegetables. The sauce can be kept covered and refrigerated for up to 3 days.

Nuoc Cham

1/3 cup	sugar (or to taste)	75 mL
1 cup	warm water	250 mL
1 or 2	small red chilies, seeded and minced (or 2 tsp [10 mL] dried chili flakes)	1 or 2
2 tbsp	white rice vinegar	25 mL
2 tbsp	fresh lime juice	25 mL
1 tbsp	minced garlic	15 mL
1/2 cup	fish sauce	125 mL
1	small carrot, peeled and finely shredded	1

1. In a small bowl, combine sugar and warm water, stirring until sugar is dissolved. Add remaining ingredients, except carrots, and mix well. Allow to stand for at least 30 minutes to develop flavors.

2. Just before serving the sauce, wrap shredded carrots in a clean towel and squeeze to remove excess moisture; add carrots to sauce.

FROM
NEW WORLD NOODLES
BY BILL JONES & STEPHEN
WONG

Serves 4 as an appetizer

The silken texture of the salmon and the crunchy noodle cake makes a great combination.

•

The components can be made well in advance. Keep the pancakes in a warm oven and assemble just before serving.

Smoked Salmon and Cream Cheese on a Crispy Noodle Pancake

PREHEAT OVEN TO 250° F (120° C)

4 oz	smoked salmon,	125 g
1 cup	cream cheese, softened	250 mL
2 tbsp	chopped chives	25 mL
4 cups	fresh chow mein noodles	1L
1 tsp	sesame oil	5 mL
1	green onion, thinly sliced	1
1 tbsp	vegetable oil	15 mL
	Salt and pepper to taste	

1. On a cutting board, stretch out 12 inches (30 cm) of plastic wrap. Lay paper-thin slices of salmon on the plastic, their edges overlapping slightly. Spread cream cheese evenly over salmon layer. Sprinkle with chopped chives. Using the plastic wrap to help you, tightly roll the salmon mixture into a log. Cut into thin slices and set aside.

2. In a heatproof bowl or pot, cover noodles with boiling water and let soak for 5 minutes. Drain and toss with sesame oil and green onions.

3. In a nonstick wok or skillet, heat oil for 30 seconds. Add half the noodles, press down with a spatula to flatten and cook on one side until golden, about 5 minutes. Flip, press down hard and cook the other side for an additional 5 minutes. Season with salt and pepper and drain on a paper towel. Keep warm in oven. Repeat procedure with remaining noodles.

4. Cut the pancakes into eighths, top each with two salmon rolls and garnish with green onion or chives.

Portobello Mushrooms with Goat Cheese

Serves 2

Exotic-sounding name notwithstanding, portobello mushrooms are nothing more than overgrown regular mushrooms. But for some alchemical reason their taste is very different (more meaty) from those lowly buttons. As a result they are usually associated with "wild" (or "fancy") mushrooms and are very much in demand. Luckily, they are available everywhere and often, quite conveniently, already trimmed and sliced into attractive 1/2-inch (1 cm) slices.

Green peppercorns are sold packed in brine; leftovers will keep if refrigerated in their original brine. While optional, they are delicious in this recipe.

FROM
SIMPLY
MEDITERRANEAN COOKING BY
BYRON AYANOGLU & ALGIS
KEMEZYS

BAKING SHEET
PREHEAT BROILER

2 tbsp	olive oil	25 mL
6 oz	portobello mushrooms, trimmed and sliced 1/2 inch (1 cm) thick	175 g
1 tbsp	finely chopped garlic	15 mL
2 tsp	balsamic vinegar	10 mL
1/4 tsp	salt	1 mL
1/8 tsp	freshly ground black pepper	0.5 mL
1/4 tsp	drained green peppercorns (optional)	1 mL
2 oz	goat cheese	50 g
2 tsp	pine nuts	10 mL
	Several lettuce leaves	
2 tsp	olive oil	10 mL

1. In a nonstick frying pan, heat 2 tbsp (25 mL) olive oil over high heat for 1 minute. Add mushroom slices in one layer; cook 2 to 3 minutes or until nicely browned (they will absorb all the oil). Turn and cook second side for under a minute. Add garlic, 1 tsp (5 mL) of the balsamic vinegar, salt and pepper; continue cooking for 1 minute to brown the garlic somewhat.

2. Remove from heat. Arrange on baking sheet in 2 flat piles about 3 inches (7.5 cm) wide. Sprinkle evenly with green peppercorns, if using. Divide the goat cheese in two; make each half into a thick disc, about 1 inch (2.5 cm) wide. Place a disc of cheese on each pile of mushrooms. Sprinkle the pine nuts evenly over the piles, some on the cheese and some on the surrounding mushrooms. (The recipe can wait at this point up to 1 hour, covered and unrefrigerated).

3. Broil the mushrooms for just under 4 minutes or until the cheese is soft and a little brown, and the pine nuts are dark brown.

4. Line 2 plates with lettuce. Carefully lift each pile off the baking sheet and transfer as intact as possible onto the lettuce. Sprinkle about 1 tsp (5 mL) olive oil and 1/2 tsp (2 mL) balsamic vinegar over each portion and serve immediately.

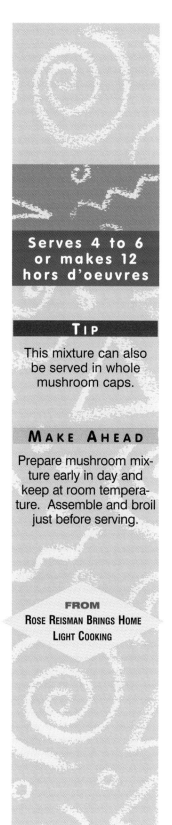

Sautéed Mushrooms on Toast Rounds

Serves 4 to 6 or makes 12 hors d'oeuvres

TIP

This mixture can also be served in whole mushroom caps.

MAKE AHEAD

Prepare mushroom mixture early in day and keep at room temperature. Assemble and broil just before serving.

FROM

ROSE REISMAN BRINGS HOME LIGHT COOKING

PREHEAT BROILER

2 tsp	vegetable oil	10 mL
1 tsp	crushed garlic	5 mL
2 tbsp	finely chopped onions	25 mL
1/2 lb	mushrooms, chopped	250 g
1 tbsp	chopped fresh parsley	15 mL
2 tbsp	white wine	25 mL
2 tbsp	chopped green onions or chives	25 mL
1 tsp	soya sauce	5 mL
2 tbsp	dry bread crumbs	25 mL
2 tbsp	grated Parmesan cheese	25 mL
	Salt and pepper	
16	slices small rye bread or French baguette	16

1. In a small nonstick saucepan, heat oil; sauté garlic, onions and mushrooms until softened, approximately 5 minutes.

2. Add parsley, wine, green onions, soya sauce, bread crumbs, 1 tbsp (15 mL) of the Parmesan, and salt and pepper to taste; cook for 2 minutes. Set aside.

3. On baking sheet, toast bread in oven just until browned on both sides, approximately 2 minutes (or brown in toaster). Divide mushroom mixture over bread; sprinkle with remaining Parmesan. Broil for 5 minutes or until hot, being careful not to burn.

TIP

For blue cheese lovers, increase to 3 oz (75 g). Instead of endive leaves, fill empty mushroom caps, or serve as a dip with crackers or vegetables.

MAKE AHEAD

Prepare dip and refrigerate up to a day before. Spoon onto endive leaves just before serving.

FROM
ROSE REISMAN BRINGS HOME LIGHT COOKING

Ricotta and Blue Cheese Appetizers

2 oz	blue cheese	50 g
1/2 cup	ricotta cheese	125 mL
2 tbsp	2% yogurt	25 mL
2 tbsp	chopped fresh dill (or 1 tsp [5 mL] dried dillweed)	25 mL
2	Belgian endives	2

1. In food processor, combine blue cheese, ricotta, yogurt and dill; process until creamy and smooth.

2. Separate Belgian endive leaves. Spoon 2 tsp (10 mL) cheese mixture onto stem end of each.

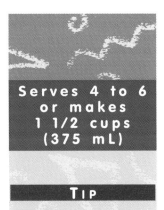

Serves 4 to 6
or makes
1 1/2 cups
(375 mL)

Spinach and Ricotta Dip

Half	pkg (10 oz [284 g]) fresh spinach	Half
1/2 cup	2% yogurt	125 mL
3/4 cup	ricotta cheese	175 mL
1/2 tsp	crushed garlic	2 mL
2 tbsp	chopped fresh parsley	25 mL
2 tbsp	grated Parmesan cheese	25 mL
	Salt and pepper	

1. Rinse spinach and shake off excess water. With just the water clinging to leaves, cook until wilted; drain and squeeze out excess moisture.

2. In food processor, combine spinach, yogurt, ricotta, garlic, parsley, Parmesan cheese, and salt and pepper to taste; process just until still chunky. Do not purée.

TIP

You can cook half a package (150 g) frozen spinach instead of the fresh, then continue with recipe.

•

An interesting way to serve this is to hollow out a small round bread or roll. Fill with dip and use bread chunks as dippers. Or serve in a decorative bowl with vegetable sticks or crackers.

MAKE AHEAD

Prepare and refrigerate up to a day before. Stir just before serving. (If filling bread, do so just prior to serving.)

FROM
ROSE REISMAN BRINGS HOME
LIGHT COOKING

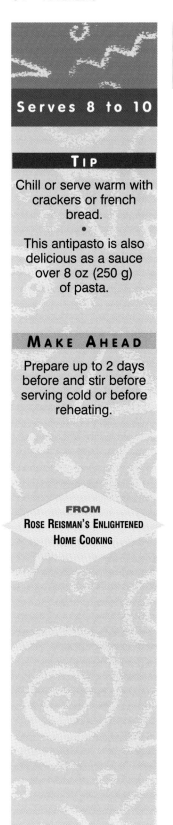

Serves 8 to 10

TIP

Chill or serve warm with crackers or french bread.

•

This antipasto is also delicious as a sauce over 8 oz (250 g) of pasta.

MAKE AHEAD

Prepare up to 2 days before and stir before serving cold or before reheating.

FROM
ROSE REISMAN'S ENLIGHTENED
HOME COOKING

Eggplant and Tuna Antipasto Appetizer

1 tbsp	olive oil	15 mL
1 1/2 cups	peeled, chopped eggplant	375 mL
1 cup	sliced mushrooms	250 mL
3/4 cup	chopped red peppers	175 mL
1/2 cup	chopped onions	125 mL
2 tsp	minced garlic	10 mL
1 tsp	dried basil	5 mL
1/2 tsp	dried oregano	2 mL
1/2 cup	chicken stock *or* water	125 mL
1/2 cup	crushed tomatoes (canned or fresh)	125 mL
1/3 cup	sliced pimiento-stuffed green olives	75 mL
1/3 cup	bottled chili sauce	75 mL
2 tsp	drained capers	10 mL
1	can (6.5 oz [184 g]) tuna in water, drained	1

1. Spray a nonstick pan with vegetable spray. Heat oil in pan over medium-high heat; add eggplant, mushrooms, red peppers, onions, garlic, basil and oregano. Cook for 8 minutes, stirring occasionally, or until vegetables are softened.

2. Add stock, tomatoes, olives, chili sauce and capers; simmer uncovered for 6 minutes, stirring occasionally until most of the liquid is absorbed.

3. Transfer to bowl of food processor and add tuna; process for 20 seconds or until combined but still chunky.

Snacks

Avocado Tomato Salsa

Serves 8

TIP

Serve with crackers or tortilla crisps.

•

For an authentic, intense flavor, use 1/2 tsp (2 mL) finely diced chili pepper, or more chili powder.

MAKE AHEAD

Prepare up to 4 hours ahead; stir before serving.

FROM
ROSE REISMAN'S ENLIGHTENED HOME COOKING

2 cups	finely chopped plum tomatoes	500 mL
1/2 cup	finely chopped ripe but firm avocado (about 1/2 avocado)	125 mL
1/3 cup	chopped fresh coriander	75 mL
1/4 cup	chopped green onions (about 2 medium)	50 mL
1 tbsp	olive oil	15 mL
1 tbsp	lime juice *or* lemon juice	15 mL
1 tsp	minced garlic	5 mL
1/8 tsp	chili powder	1 mL

1. In a serving bowl, combine tomatoes, avocado, coriander, green onions, olive oil, lime juice, garlic and chili powder; let marinate 1 hour before serving.

Bagel Garlic Bread

PREHEAT OVEN TO 350° F (180° C)

2	bagels	2
1 tbsp	margarine, melted	15 mL
1/2 tsp	crushed garlic	2 mL
1 1/2 tsp	grated Parmesan cheese	7 mL
1 tbsp	chopped fresh parsley	15 mL

1. Slice each bagel into 6 very thin rounds.
2. In bowl, combine margarine, garlic, cheese and parsley until well mixed. Brush over bagel rounds. Bake on baking sheet until crisp, 10 to 14 minutes.

Bruschetta with Basil and Oregano

PREHEAT BROILER

2	small tomatoes, diced	2
2 tbsp	olive oil	25 mL
1 tsp	crushed garlic	5 mL
2 tbsp	chopped fresh basil (or 1 tsp [5 mL] dried)	25 mL
1 tbsp	chopped fresh oregano (or 1/2 tsp [2 mL] dried)	15 mL
1 tbsp	chopped green onion	15 mL
12	slices (1/2-inch [1 cm] thick) French bread	12
1 tbsp	grated Parmesan cheese	15 mL

1. In a small bowl, combine tomatoes, oil, garlic, basil, oregano and onion. Let stand for at least 20 minutes.
2. Toast bread on baking sheet under broiler, turning once, until brown on both sides. Divide tomato mixture over bread; sprinkle with cheese. Broil for 2 minutes or until heated through.

English Muffin Tomato Olive Bruschetta

Serves 8

TIP

Instead of using your toaster, toast the muffin halves on a baking sheet 3 inches (7.5 cm) under a preheated broiler for 2 minutes.

•

To avoid excess liquid, remove seeds from tomatoes. Plum tomatoes will give a firmer texture.

MAKE AHEAD

You can make the tomato mixture a few hours ahead, but don't top the muffins until you're ready to bake and serve.

FROM
ROSE REISMAN'S ENLIGHTENED HOME COOKING

PREHEAT OVEN TO 450°C (230°C)

2 cups	diced tomatoes (2 medium), preferably plum	500 mL
2 tbsp	olive oil	25 mL
3 tbsp	chopped fresh basil (or 1 tsp [5 mL] dried)	45 mL
1 tsp	minced garlic	5 mL
1/4 cup	chopped black olives	50 mL
4	English muffins	4
1 oz	goat cheese	25 g

1. In a bowl combine tomatoes, olive oil, basil, garlic and olives; set aside.

2. Split and toast English muffins and place on baking sheet. Top each muffin half with 1/4 cup (50 mL) of the tomato mixture. Crumble the goat cheese and sprinkle over top of muffins.

3. Bake for 5 minutes or until cheese melts and topping is warmed through. Cut in quarters and serve.

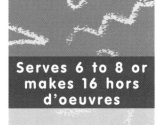

TIP

Any combination of vegetables can be used, as well as any type of cheese. Goat cheese is exceptional on pizzas. Try 1/4 cup (50 mL) chopped sun-dried tomatoes.

MAKE AHEAD

Prepare pizzas early in day and refrigerate. Bake just before serving.

FROM
ROSE REISMAN BRINGS HOME LIGHT COOKING

Pita or Tortilla Pizzas

PREHEAT OVEN TO 400° F (200° C)

3/4 cup	tomato sauce	175 mL
4	flour tortillas *or* pita breads (preferably whole wheat)	4
8	small mushrooms, thinly sliced	8
1/4 cup	diced sweet red or green pepper	50 mL
1 tbsp	chopped fresh basil (or 1 tsp [5 mL] dried)	15 mL
1/2 tsp	dried oregano	2 mL
1 cup	shredded mozzarella cheese	250 mL
1/4 cup	chopped feta cheese (optional)	50 mL

1. Divide tomato sauce among breads; spread evenly.
2. Top with mushrooms, red pepper, basil and oregano. Sprinkle with cheese.
3. Bake for 12 minutes or until crisp and cheese is melted. Cut each into 4 pieces.

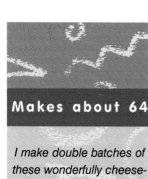

Makes about 64

I make double batches of these wonderfully cheese-laden sticks, especially at holiday time. They are perfect as appetizers and great to serve along with soup. To obtain the richest flavor, buy a wedge of authentic Parmigiano Reggiano and have it finely grated for you at the cheese shop.

TIP

Baked straws can be stored in covered container for up to 5 days. Or freeze unbaked straws for up to 2 months in a covered container lined with waxed paper. No need to defrost before baking.

FROM
THE COMFORT FOOD COOKBOOK BY JOHANNA BURKHARD

Nippy Parmesan Cheese Straws

PREHEAT OVEN TO 375° F (190° C)
BAKING SHEET(S) LINED WITH PARCHMENT PAPER

1 cup	freshly grated Parmesan cheese	250 mL
1/2 tsp	sweet Hungarian paprika	2 mL
1/4 tsp	cayenne pepper	1 mL
1	pkg (1 lb [400 g]) puff pastry (2 sheets)	1

1. In a bowl combine Parmesan, paprika and cayenne pepper.

2. Sprinkle work surface with 2 tbsp (25 mL) of the Parmesan mixture to cover an area approximately the same size as 1 pastry sheet. Place pastry sheet to cover sprinkled Parmesan mixture; sprinkle top of sheet with another 2 tbsp (25 mL) of the Parmesan mixture.

3. Roll out pastry to make a 10-inch (25 cm) square. Sprinkle half the pastry with 2 tbsp (25 mL) of the Parmesan mixture; fold dough over in half. Sprinkle with 2 tbsp (25 mL) more Parmesan mixture. Roll out to make a thin 12- by 10-inch (30 by 25 cm) rectangle. Cut dough in half to make two 12- by 5-inch (30 by 12.5 cm) rectangles.

4. With a sharp knife and using a ruler as a guide, cut pastry into strips measuring 5 by 3/4 inches (13 by 2 cm); twist each strip 3 or 4 times to make a spiral. Arrange on parchment paper-lined baking sheets, pressing the ends onto the sheets to hold them in place.

5. Repeat steps 2 through 4 with second pastry sheet and remaining Parmesan mixture.

6. Freeze for 15 minutes or until pastry is firm. Bake in preheated oven for 14 to 16 minutes or until puffed and golden. Transfer to a rack to cool.

Salmon Swiss Cheese English Muffins

Serves 8 or makes 32 wedges

TIP

Tuna packed in water is a great substitute for salmon.

•

You can also use the mixture as a dip if you purée it until smooth. Serve 2 whole halves as a light lunch.

MAKE AHEAD

Make and refrigerate salmon mixture up to a day before. Stir before spreading on muffins.

FROM
ROSE REISMAN BRINGS HOME
LIGHT COOKING

PREHEAT BROILER

1	can (7 1/2 oz [220 g]) salmon, drained	1
1/4 cup	light mayonnaise	50 mL
2 tbsp	chopped green onion	25 mL
2 tbsp	chopped red onion	25 mL
2 tbsp	diced celery	25 mL
2 tbsp	chopped fresh dill (or 1 tsp [5 mL] dried dillweed)	25 mL
2 tsp	lemon juice	10 mL
4	English muffins, split in half and toasted	4
1/3 cup	shredded Swiss cheese	75 mL

1. In food processor, combine salmon, mayonnaise, green and red onions, celery, dill and lemon juice. Using on/off motion, process just until chunky but not puréed.

2. Divide salmon mixture over muffins and spread evenly. Sprinkle with cheese. Broil just until cheese melts, approximately 2 minutes. To serve, slice each muffin into quarters.

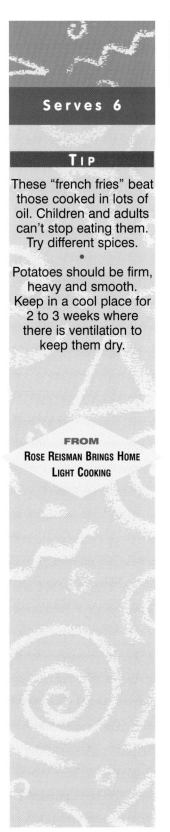

TIP

These "french fries" beat those cooked in lots of oil. Children and adults can't stop eating them. Try different spices.

•

Potatoes should be firm, heavy and smooth. Keep in a cool place for 2 to 3 weeks where there is ventilation to keep them dry.

FROM
ROSE REISMAN BRINGS HOME
LIGHT COOKING

Baked French Wedge Potatoes

PREHEAT OVEN TO 375° F (190° C)
BAKING SHEET SPRAYED WITH VEGETABLE SPRAY

4	medium potatoes, unpeeled	4
2 tbsp	margarine, melted	25 mL
1/2 tsp	chili powder	2 mL
1/2 tsp	dried basil	2 mL
1 tsp	crushed garlic	5 mL
1 1/2 tsp	chopped fresh parsley	7 mL
1 tbsp	grated Parmesan cheese	15 mL

1. Scrub potatoes; cut each into 8 wedges. Place on baking sheet.

2. In a small bowl, combine margarine, chili powder, basil, garlic and parsley; brush half over potatoes. Sprinkle with half of the Parmesan; bake for 30 minutes. Turn wedges over; brush with remaining mixture and sprinkle with remaining cheese. Bake for 30 minutes longer.

Goat Cheese and Tomato Salad Wraps

Serves 4

4 oz	goat cheese, crumbled	125 g
1 1/4 cups	diced seeded tomatoes	300 mL
1 1/4 cups	diced cucumbers	300 mL
1/2 cup	chopped green onions	125 mL
2 tsp	olive oil	10 mL
2 tsp	balsamic vinegar	10 mL
4	10-inch (25 cm) flour tortillas, preferably different flavors, if available	4

1. In a bowl combine goat cheese, tomatoes, cucumbers, green onions, oil and vinegar. Divide mixture equally between tortillas.

2. Form each tortilla into a packet by folding bottom edge over filling, then sides, then top, to enclose filling completely.

TIP

Flavored tortillas — such as pesto, sun-dried tomato, herb or whole wheat — are now appearing in many supermarkets. Using different flavors will add taste variety and visual interest to these wraps.

•

Plum tomatoes provide a firmer texture and less excess liquid.

•

If 10-inch (25 cm) tortillas are unavailable, use a smaller size and make 6 wraps.

MAKE AHEAD

Prepare vegetables early in day, but don't combine until just before serving.

FROM
ROSE REISMAN'S LIGHT VEGETARIAN COOKING

TIP

Use a firm-fleshed white fish, cut into strips, instead of chicken.

•

About 3 cups (750 mL) corn flakes equals 1 cup (250 mL) crushed flakes.

MAKE AHEAD

These "fingers" can be coated early in the day and refrigerated. Bake before serving. Also excellent if gently reheated. These can be frozen and reheated for children's meals.

FROM
ROSE REISMAN'S ENLIGHTENED
HOME COOKING

Honey Coated Crunchy Chicken Fingers

PREHEAT OVEN TO 425° F (220° C)
BAKING SHEET SPRAYED WITH VEGETABLE SPRAY

1 lb	skinless boneless chicken breasts	500 g
1/4 cup	honey (slightly warmed)	50 mL
1/4 cup	water	50 mL
1 cup	crushed corn flakes	250 mL

1. Cut chicken breasts crosswise into strips 3/4 inch (2 cm) wide. In small bowl combine honey and water. Put corn flakes on a plate.

2. Dip chicken strips in honey mixture then coat with corn flake crumbs. Put on prepared baking sheet. Bake for 10 minutes, or until cooked at center, turning chicken over at halfway point.

Tuna and White Bean Spread

1 cup	canned, cooked white kidney beans, drained	250 mL
1	can (6.5 oz [184 g]) tuna in water, drained	1
1 1/2 tsp	minced garlic	7 mL
2 tbsp	lemon juice	25 mL
2 tbsp	light mayonnaise	25 mL
1/4 cup	5% ricotta cheese	50 mL
3 tbsp	minced red onions	45 mL
1/4 cup	minced fresh dill (or 1 tsp [5 mL] dried)	50 mL
1 tbsp	grated Parmesan cheese	15 mL
1/4 cup	diced red pepper	50 mL

1. Place beans, tuna, garlic, lemon juice, mayonnaise and ricotta in food processor; pulse on and off until combined but still chunky. Place in serving bowl.

2. Stir onions, dill, Parmesan and red pepper into bean mixture.

Hot Beef Subs

4	crusty submarine rolls	4
1/4 cup	light cream cheese, softened	50 mL
2 tbsp	mayonnaise	25 mL
2 tbsp	Dijon mustard	25 mL
2	tomatoes, thinly sliced	2
1 tbsp	olive oil	15 mL
1	small red onion, thinly sliced	1
1	large clove garlic, minced	1
1 cup	sliced mushrooms	250 mL
Half	large sweet green pepper, cut into thin 1 1/2 inches (4 cm) strips	Half
1/2 tsp	dried oregano	2 mL
1 cup	thin strips cooked flank steak *or* round steak	250 mL
	Salt and pepper	

1. Split rolls along 1 side and open; grill or broil cut sides until toasted.

2. In a bowl, blend cream cheese, mayonnaise and mustard; spread over cut sides of rolls. Line with tomato slices. Set aside.

3. In a large nonstick skillet, heat oil over medium-high heat. Add onion, garlic, mushrooms, green pepper and oregano; cook, stirring often, for 3 to 5 minutes.

4. Add beef; cook, stirring, for 1 minute more or until hot. Season with salt and pepper to taste. Spoon into rolls; serve immediately.

Broccoli and Cheese-Stuffed Potatoes

Serves 4

TIP

Cheddar and broccoli are a classic combo, but get adventurous with whatever cheese and vegetables are in the fridge. Another favorite is mozzarella cheese and lightly sautéed mushrooms and diced red peppers seasoned with basil.

How to bake potatoes
Scrub baking potatoes (10 oz [300 g] each) well and pierce skins with a fork in several places to allow steam to escape.

To oven bake: Place in 400° F (200° C) oven for 1 hour or until potatoes give slightly when squeezed.

To microwave: Arrange potatoes in a circle, spacing 1-inch (2.5 cm) apart on roasting rack or on a paper towel in microwave oven. Microwave at High, turning over halfway through cooking, until potatoes are just tender when pierced with a skewer.

Microwave cooking times at High: 1 potato, 4 to 5 minutes; 2 potatoes, 6 to 8 minutes; 4 potatoes, 10 to 12 minutes
•
For moist potatoes wrap cooked potatoes individually in foil. For drier potatoes, wrap in a dry towel. Let stand 5 minutes.

FROM
THE COMFORT FOOD COOKBOOK BY JOHANNA BURKHARD

These delicious baked potatoes are great to pack along to work if you have the use of a microwave for reheating.

PREHEAT OVEN TO 400° F (200° C)
SHALLOW BAKING DISH

4	large baking potatoes (about 10 oz [300 g] each)	4
3 cups	small broccoli florets and peeled, chopped stems	750 mL
1/2 cup	sour cream *or* plain yogurt *or* buttermilk (approximate)	125 mL
2	green onions, chopped	2
1 1/3 cups	shredded Cheddar or Gruyere cheese	325 mL
	Salt and cayenne pepper	

1. Bake or microwave potatoes as directed (see Tip, at left).

2. In a saucepan cook or steam broccoli until just crisp-tender. (Or place in covered casserole and microwave at High for 3 minutes.) Drain well.

3. Cut a thin slice from tops of warm potatoes. Scoop out potato leaving a 1/4-inch (5 mm) shell, being careful not to tear the skins.

4. In a bowl mash potato with potato masher or fork; beat in enough sour cream until smooth. Add broccoli, onion and 1 cup (250 mL) of the cheese. Season with salt and a dash of cayenne pepper to taste.

5. Spoon filling into potato shells, mounding the tops. Arrange in shallow baking dish; sprinkle with remaining cheese. Bake in preheated oven for 20 minutes or until cheese melts. Or place on a rack and microwave at Medium-High for 5 to 7 minutes or until heated through and cheese melts.

TIP

Children often prefer this sauce smoother. If too chunky, run through the food processor.
If a livelier taste is desired, use spicy sausage.

•

This recipe can also be used as a pasta sauce.

MAKE AHEAD

Can be made up to 2 days ahead or frozen for up to 3 weeks. Great as leftovers.

FROM
ROSE REISMAN'S ENLIGHTENED HOME COOKING

Beef and Sausage Sloppy Joes

2 tsp	vegetable oil	10 mL
1 cup	chopped onions	250 mL
2 tsp	minced garlic	10 mL
8 oz	lean ground beef	250 g
8 oz	mild Italian sausage, chopped, casings removed	250 g
4 cups	chopped fresh tomatoes (or 28 oz [796 mL] can, drained, chopped tomatoes)	1 L
1 1/2 tsp	dried basil	7 mL
1 tsp	chili powder	5 mL
1/2 tsp	dried oregano	2 mL
2 tbsp	grated Parmesan cheese (optional)	25 mL

1. In large nonstick skillet, heat oil over medium heat; add onions and garlic and cook for 4 minutes or until softened. Add ground beef and sausage and cook for 5 minutes, breaking up meat with a spoon, or until no longer pink. Drain off excess fat.

2. Add tomatoes, basil, chili powder and oregano; bring to a boil, reduce heat to low and simmer uncovered for 30 minutes, stirring occasionally. Serve over toasted hamburger buns. Sprinkle with Parmesan cheese if desired.

Avocado, Tomato and Chili Guacamole

Serves 4 to 6
or makes
3/4 cup (175 mL)

TIP

Adjust the chili powder,
to your taste.
Serve with pita bread,
vegetables or crackers.

MAKE AHEAD

Make early in day and
squeeze more lemon
juice over top to prevent
discoloration.
Refrigerate. Stir just
before serving.

FROM
ROSE REISMAN BRINGS HOME
LIGHT COOKING

Half	avocado, peeled	Half
3/4 tsp	crushed garlic	4 mL
2 tbsp	chopped green onions	25 mL
1 tbsp	lemon juice	15 mL
1/4 cup	finely diced sweet red pepper	50 mL
1/2 cup	chopped tomato	125 mL
Pinch	chili powder	Pinch

1. In a bowl, combine avocado, garlic, onions, lemon juice, red pepper, tomato and chili powder; mash with fork, mixing well.

Chunky Sun-Dried Tomato and Goat Cheese Spread

PREHEAT OVEN TO 425° F (220° C)

1/2 cup	sun-dried tomatoes (dry, not marinated in oil)	125 mL
1/3 cup	chopped black olives	75 mL
2 tbsp	grated Parmesan cheese	25 mL
1 tbsp	olive oil	15 mL
2 tbsp	water	25 mL
1 1/2 tsp	minced garlic	7 mL
5	English muffins	5
1 oz	goat cheese	25 g

1. Pour boiling water over sun-dried tomatoes. Let sit for 15 minutes, drain and chop.

2. Place sun dried tomatoes, olives, Parmesan, olive oil, water and garlic in bowl of food processor; pulse until combined, but still chunky.

3. Split muffins and toast them in toaster or oven; spread each muffin half with approximately 1 tbsp (15 mL) of tomato mixture. Crumble goat cheese and sprinkle over top of muffins.

4. Bake for 5 minutes or until cheese melts and muffins are heated through. Cut in quarters and serve.

Sweet Potato Fries with Cinnamon and Maple Syrup

Serves 4

TIP

The maple syrup gives an unusual sweet taste. For a stronger flavor, use half molasses and half maple syrup. Honey can also be used.

MAKE AHEAD

Cut and brush potatoes with maple syrup mixture early in the day. Bake just before serving.

FROM
ROSE REISMAN'S ENLIGHTENED HOME COOKING

PREHEAT OVEN TO 375° F (190° C)
BAKING SHEET SPRAYED WITH VEGETABLE SPRAY

2	large sweet potatoes, unpeeled	2
1 1/2 tbsp	melted margarine *or* butter	20 mL
3 tsp	maple syrup	15 mL
3/4 tsp	cinnamon	4 mL
1/4 tsp	ginger	1 mL
Pinch	nutmeg	Pinch

1. Scrub sweet potatoes and cut lengthwise into 8 wedges. Place on prepared baking sheet.

2. In small bowl, combine margarine, maple syrup, cinnamon, ginger and nutmeg; brush half over the potato wedges. Bake for 20 minutes. Turn wedges over and brush with remaining mixture. Bake for 20 minutes longer, or until tender.

Serves 4
Makes 10 latkes

TIP

Although these vegetable patties are delicious on their own, a simple sauce can be made for them by whisking together 1/2 cup (125 mL) light sour cream and 1 tbsp (15 mL) chopped fresh dill.

•

These latkes taste great the next day reheated. Prepare in 2 batches if necessary.

MAKE AHEAD

Prepare mixture early in the day, make into patties and refrigerate until ready to bake.

FROM
ROSE REISMAN'S ENLIGHTENED
HOME COOKING

Vegetable Dill Latkes
(Pancakes)

Serves 4
Makes 10 latkes

PREHEAT OVEN TO 375° F (190° C)
BAKING SHEET SPRAYED WITH VEGETABLE SPRAY

1 1/4 cups	diced zucchini, unpeeled	300 mL
1 1/4 cups	diced peeled sweet potatoes	300 mL
3/4 cup	diced peeled carrots	175 mL
1/3 cup	diced onions	75 mL
2	eggs	2
1/3 cup	chopped fresh dill (or 2 tsp [10 mL] dried)	75 mL
1 tsp	minced garlic	5 mL
1 cup	all-purpose flour	250 mL
1/2 tsp	baking powder	2 mL
1/4 tsp	salt	1 mL
1/4 tsp	ground black pepper	1 mL

1. In food processor, combine zucchini, sweet potatoes, carrots, onions, eggs, dill and garlic; process on and off until well combined. In small bowl, stir together flour, baking powder, salt and pepper. Add flour mixture to vegetable mixture, process on and off just until combined.

2. Scoop 1/4 cup (50 mL) of batter into your hands and shape into a patty; put on prepared baking sheet. Repeat until all batter has been used. Bake for 10 minutes, turn over and bake for 10 minutes more.

Salads

Serves 6

The king of tossed salads was named after a Tijuana restaurateur by the name of Caesar Cardini. Here, mayonnaise gives this classic salad an even creamier texture than the original.

TIP

Raw or coddled eggs are considered taboo in salads because they may contain salmonella bacteria. Mayonnaise is used instead.

•

Make sure salad greens are washed and dried thoroughly, preferably in a salad spinner, for best results. Homemade croutons make a definite flavor difference but 3 cups (750 mL) store-bought croutons work in a pinch.

•

Anchovy fillets are best, but 1 tbsp (15 mL) anchovy paste can be used instead.

FROM
THE COMFORT FOOD
COOKBOOK BY JOHANNA
BURKHARD

Caesar Salad

1/3 cup	olive oil	75 mL
2 tbsp	mayonnaise	25 mL
2 tbsp	fresh lemon juice	25 mL
2 tbsp	water	25 mL
1 tsp	Dijon mustard	5 mL
2	cloves garlic, finely chopped	2
3	anchovy fillets, chopped	3
1/4 tsp	pepper	1 mL
1	large head Romaine lettuce, torn into bite-sized pieces (about 12 cups [3 L])	1
6	slices bacon, cooked crisp and crumbled (optional)	6
	Garlic croutons (recipe, page 60)	
1/3 cup	freshly grated Parmesan cheese	75 mL
	Salt	

1. In a food processor, combine oil, mayonnaise, lemon juice, water, mustard, garlic, anchovy fillets and pepper; process until smooth and creamy.

2. Arrange lettuce in salad bowl; pour dressing over and toss lightly. Add croutons; sprinkle with crumbled bacon, is using, and Parmesan cheese. Toss again. Taste and season with salt and pepper, if needed. Serve immediately.

FROM
THE COMFORT FOOD
COOKBOOK BY JOHANNA
BURKHARD

Garlic Croutons

PREHEAT OVEN TO 375° F (190° C)

4 cups	cubed crusty bread, cut into 1/2-inch (1 cm) pieces	1 L
2 tbsp	olive oil	25 mL
1	clove garlic, minced	1
2 tbsp	freshly grated Parmesan cheese	25 mL

1. Place bread cubes in a bowl. Combine oil and garlic; drizzle over bread cubes and toss. Sprinkle with Parmesan and toss again. Arrange on baking sheet in single layer. Toast in preheated oven, stirring once, for about 10 minutes or until golden.

Asian Caesar Salad

This is a simple and delicious rendition of an all-time favorite. The oyster sauce stands in for traditional anchovies and complements the garlic. You can easily transform this into a main course by adding slices of grilled vegetables, smoked salmon, cooked chicken, beef or seafood.

FROM
NEW WORLD CHINESE COOKING BY BILL JONES & STEPHEN WONG

Dressing

4 tbsp	light mayonnaise	60 mL
2 tbsp	oyster sauce	25 mL
1 tbsp	minced garlic	15 mL
1 tbsp	lemon juice	15 mL
1 tbsp	rice vinegar	15 mL
1 tbsp	chopped cilantro	15 mL
	Salt and pepper to taste	

Salad

1	head romaine lettuce, washed	1
1	red or yellow bell pepper, seeded and cut into 1/2-inch (1 cm) dice	1
1 cup	diced seedless cucumbers	250 mL
1	green onion, thinly sliced	1
	Sesame seeds for garnish	
	Freshly ground black pepper to taste	

1. In a small bowl, combine mayonnaise, oyster sauce, garlic, lemon juice, vinegar and cilantro. Season with salt and pepper; whisk until well mixed.

2. Remove root end from lettuce and wash leaves well under cold water. Tear lettuce into pieces, approximately 2 inches (5 cm) square and dry in a salad spinner or by wrapping in a clean, dry kitchen cloth. Refrigerate at least 15 minutes.

3. In a large salad bowl, combine lettuce, red or yellow bell pepper, cucumbers and green onion. Top with dressing; toss. Serve on individual salad plates with a generous sprinkling of sesame seeds and a grind of fresh pepper.

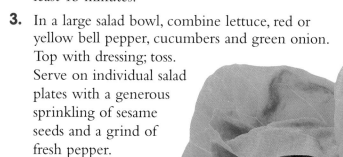

TIP

Substitute other vegeta-bles for those listed. Try asparagus instead of snow peas, yellow or green pepper instead of red pepper, or choose other lettuces.

MAKE AHEAD

Prepare dressing up to a day before. Toss with salad just before serving.

FROM
ROSE REISMAN BRINGS HOME
LIGHT COOKING

Broccoli, Snow Pea and Baby Corn Salad with Orange Dressing

2 cups	chopped broccoli florets	500 mL
1 cup	snow peas, cut into pieces	250 mL
1/2 cup	sliced onion	125 mL
Half	medium sweet red pepper, sliced	Half
3 cups	torn romaine lettuce	750 mL
3/4 cup	drained mandarin orange sections	175 mL
1/2 cup	sliced water chestnuts	125 mL
8	drained canned baby corn cobs	8
1 tbsp	raisins	15 mL
1 tbsp	chopped walnuts	15 mL

Dressing

3 tbsp	olive oil	45 mL
3 tbsp	frozen orange juice concentrate, thawed	45 mL
1 1/2 tsp	red wine vinegar	7 mL
1/2 tsp	crushed garlic	2 mL
4 tsp	lemon juice	20 mL
1 tsp	granulated sugar	5 mL

1. Steam or microwave broccoli and snow peas just until tender-crisp. Drain and rinse with cold water; drain again and pat dry. Place in serving bowl.

2. Add onion, red pepper, lettuce, oranges, water chest-nuts, corn, raisins and walnuts.

3. Dressing: In small bowl, mix oil, orange juice concen-trate, vinegar, garlic, lemon juice and sugar; pour over salad and toss well.

FROM
ROSE REISMAN BRINGS HOME
LIGHT COOKING

Serves 4 to 6

TIP

Fresh tuna, either grilled or broiled, is fabulous. Or try grilled swordfish or shark.

MAKE AHEAD

Prepare salad and dressing early in day, but toss together just before serving.

Salade Niçoise

4 oz	green beans, trimmed	125 g
4 cups	torn leaf lettuce	1 L
2	small potatoes, peeled, cooked and chopped	2
1 cup	chopped tomatoes	250 mL
3/4 cup	chopped sweet red pepper	175 mL
1/2 cup	sliced red onions	125 mL
2	anchovies, minced	2
1	can (7 oz [213 g]) tuna (packed in water), drained and flaked	1
1/2 cup	black olives, pitted and sliced	125 mL
2 tbsp	chopped fresh parsley	25 mL
1/4 cup	chopped fresh dill (or 1 1/2 tsp [7 mL] dried dillweed)	50 mL

Dressing

2 tbsp	water	25 mL
2 tbsp	red wine vinegar	25 mL
2 tbsp	lemon juice	25 mL
1 tsp	crushed garlic	5 mL
1 tsp	Dijon mustard	5 mL
3 tbsp	vegetable oil	45 mL

1. In saucepan of boiling water, blanch green beans just until bright green. Drain and rinse with cold water. Drain and set aside.

2. Place lettuce in large salad bowl. Add green beans, potatoes, tomatoes, red pepper, onion, anchovies, tuna, olives, parsley and dill.

3. Dressing: In small bowl, combine water, vinegar, lemon juice, garlic and mustard; gradually whisk in oil until combined. Pour over salad and toss gently.

Potato and Tuna Salad

1 lb	potatoes, scrubbed	500 g
2 tbsp	white wine vinegar	25 mL
1/2 tsp	salt	2 mL
1/4 tsp	freshly ground black pepper	1 mL
Half	green pepper, thinly sliced	Half
1 cup	thinly sliced red onions	250 mL
2	stalks celery, diced	2
1/4 cup	extra virgin olive oil	50 mL
1 tbsp	drained capers	15 mL
2	cans (each 6.5 oz [184 g]) chunk light tuna, drained	2
1 tsp	vegetable oil	5 mL
1/2 cup	whole pecans (about 2 oz [50 g])	125 mL
2 tbsp	extra virgin olive oil (optional)	25 mL
	Several sprigs fresh parsley, chopped	

Serves 4 to 6

In this recipe we take two all-time favorite picnic salads, rejuvenating both while creating a brand new salad in the process. The difference here is in the treatment of potato and tuna — both are presented in large chunks and mayo-free, thereby allowing us to enjoy texture as well as taste. If you wish, substitute the canned tuna with 8 oz (250 g) fresh tuna, grilled or sautéed and cut into 1/2-inch (1 cm) strips. Just make sure that you eat the salad soon after it's made — otherwise the cooked fresh tuna will turn fishy-tasting.

A number of complementary ingredients can be served alongside this salad for more festive occasions: hard-boiled halved eggs; wedges of fresh tomato; cucumber slices; olives; and even slices of your favorite fresh fruit.

FROM
SIMPLY MEDITERRANEAN
COOKING BY BYRON AYANOGLU
& ALGIS KEMEZYS

1. Boil whole potatoes in salted water until easily pierceable, but before they start to crumble, about 30 minutes. Drain and cut while hot into 1/2-inch (1 cm) cubes. Transfer to a bowl; sprinkle evenly with vinegar, salt and pepper; toss gently to combine.

2. Add pepper slices, onions and celery; toss to combine. Add 1/4 cup (50 mL) olive oil and the capers; toss gently but thoroughly until combined. Add tuna; toss lightly to distribute the pieces but without mashing them at all. Transfer the tossed salad to a serving dish.

3. In a small frying pan, heat oil over high heat; add pecans and cook 2 to 3 minutes, turning them continuously to ensure they are browned but not burned. Decorate the salad with the fried pecans. If desired — that is, if calories are not a concern — drizzle 2 tbsp (25 mL) olive oil evenly over the salad.

4. Serve salad immediately or keep refrigerated for several hours. (Before serving, let it come to room temperature and toss it lightly so that it re-absorbs its dressing.) Garnish liberally with chopped parsley.

Sautéed Mushrooms on Wilted Greens

Serves 8

This concoction of garlicky, succulent mushrooms served over your preferred greens makes a simple but deluxe first course for important dinners. It's fast, it's yummy, and it will quickly become your favorite — as it is mine. The crucial element of this dish is the quality of the mushrooms. Ordinary mushrooms will work in a pinch, but the luxurious texture and flavor of oyster or portobello mushrooms justifies the extra cost. This recipe can be easily halved for smaller gatherings.

TIP

If desired, use 1 lb (500 g) whole oyster mushrooms, trimmed, instead of the portobello mushroom strips.

FROM
THE NEW VEGETARIAN GOURMET BY BYRON AYANOGLU

1 lb	lettuce (one type or mixture of several types), washed, dried and torn into bite-size pieces	500 g
6 tbsp	olive oil	90 mL
1/2 tsp	salt	2 mL
1/2 tsp	black pepper	2 mL
3/4 cup	thinly sliced red onions	175 mL
4 cups	thickly sliced portobello mushrooms	1 L
6	cloves garlic, finely chopped	6
2 tbsp	lemon juice	25 mL
2 tbsp	white wine	25 mL
1	medium tomato, cut in wedges	1
1/4	red pepper, cut into thin half-rounds	1/4
1 tbsp	lemon zest	15 mL
	Few sprigs fresh parsley, roughly chopped	

1. Place lettuce in a large salad bowl.

2. In a large frying pan heat olive oil over high heat. Add salt and pepper and stir. Add sliced red onions and stir-fry for 1 minute. Add mushrooms and stir-fry actively for 4 to 5 minutes, until they are shiny and beginning to char slightly. Add garlic and stir-fry for 1 minute. Add lemon juice and let come to a sizzle, about 30 seconds. Add wine and stir-fry for 1 to 2 minutes, until a syrupy sauce has formed.

3. Transfer the contents of the frying pan with all its juices, evenly over the lettuce. Use a fork to arrange the mushrooms decoratively. Garnish with tomato wedges, red pepper crescents and lemon zest. Top with some chopped parsley, and serve immediately. Toss gently at table, leaving most of the mushrooms on top.

Rapini with Balsamic Vinegar

Serves 4

1	bunch rapini, washed, bottom 1 1/2 inches (3 cm) of stalks trimmed	1
1 tsp	salt	5 mL
3 tbsp	balsamic vinegar	45 mL
2 tbsp	extra virgin olive oil	25 mL
	Black pepper to taste	
	Few sprigs fresh basil or parsley, chopped	
1/4 cup	thinly sliced red onions	50 mL
1 tsp	drained capers	5 mL
3 tbsp	shaved Parmesan or Pecorino cheese	45 mL

Some of the healthiest vegetables are also the least popular — particularly bitter greens like dandelions and rapini. Why? Mostly because they are so often treated like spinach, steamed slightly and served either plain or buttered as a side vegetable. Done that way they taste like poison. To see see how bitter greens can be made delicious we must look to the Italians, who use their unrivaled condiments and cheeses to create just the kind of culinary sorcery needed to make the greens pleasurable. These enhancements — which include olive oil, balsamic vinegar and Parmesan cheese — lend flavors and qualities that work with the bitterness and make it interesting.

1. Prepare the rapini. Cut off the top 2 1/2 inches (6 cm) — the part that has the leaves and the flowers — and set aside. Cut the remaining stalks into 1-inch (2.5 cm) pieces.

2. In a large pot, bring 1 1/2 inches (3 cm) of water to a boil. Add the salt and chopped stalks and cook uncovered for 8 minutes, until tender. Add the reserved tops and cook for another 8 minutes, uncovered. Drain, refresh with cold water, and drain again.

3. Transfer the drained rapini to a serving plate and spread out. In a small bowl combine vinegar, olive oil, pepper to taste and chopped basil or parsley. Evenly dress the rapini with this sauce. Scatter slices of red onion and capers over the rapini, and top with shaved cheese.

TIP

This salad can be served immediately, or it can wait, covered and unrefrigerated for up to 1 hour.

FROM
THE NEW VEGETARIAN
GOURMET BY BYRON
AYANOGLU

TIP

A combination of red and white cabbage is attractive.

•

For curry lovers, 1 tsp (5 mL) curry powder can be added to the dressing.

MAKE AHEAD

Prepare and refrigerate early in day and stir well before serving.

FROM
ROSE REISMAN BRINGS HOME
LIGHT COOKING

Creamy Coleslaw with Apples and Raisins

1	medium carrot, diced	1
1/3 cup	finely chopped red onion	75 mL
1/2 cup	finely chopped sweet red or green pepper	125 mL
2	green onions, diced	2
3 cups	thinly sliced white or red cabbage	750 mL
1/3 cup	diced (unpeeled) apple	75 mL
1/3 cup	raisins	75 mL

Dressing

1/4 cup	light mayonnaise	50 mL
2 tbsp	2% yogurt	25 mL
2 tbsp	lemon juice	25 mL
1 1/2 tsp	honey	7 mL
	Salt and pepper	

1. In serving bowl, combine carrot, red onion, red pepper, green onions, cabbage, apple and raisins.

2. Dressing: In small bowl, stir together mayonnaise, yogurt, lemon juice, honey, and salt and pepper to taste, mixing well. Pour over salad and toss gently to combine.

Serves 6

TIP

Great variation on traditional Greek salad. Remove seeds of tomatoes to eliminate excess liquid.

MAKE AHEAD

Prepare early in the day and refrigerate until ready to use.

FROM
ROSE REISMAN'S ENLIGHTENED HOME COOKING

Greek Barley Salad

3 cups	chicken stock *or* water	750 mL
3/4 cup	barley	175 mL
1 1/2 cups	diced cucumbers	375 mL
1 1/2 cups	diced tomatoes	375 mL
3/4 cup	chopped red onions	175 mL
3/4 cup	chopped green peppers	175 mL
1/3 cup	sliced black olives	75 mL
2 oz	feta cheese, crumbled	50 g
Dressing		
2 tbsp	olive oil	25 mL
2 tbsp	lemon juice	25 mL
1 1/2 tsp	minced garlic	7 mL
1/3 cup	chopped fresh oregano (or 2 tsp [10 mL] dried)	75 mL

1. In a medium saucepan, bring stock or water to the boil; add barley. Cover, reduce heat and simmer for 40 to 45 minutes, or just until tender. Drain well, rinse with cold water and place in large serving bowl, along with cucumbers, tomatoes, red onions, green peppers, black olives and feta cheese; toss well.

2. In a small bowl, whisk together oil, lemon juice, garlic and oregano; pour over salad and toss well. Refrigerate until chilled.

TIP

Any combination of tomatoes can be used if those specified here are not available.
•
Yellow, larger tomatoes, if available, are great to add.
•
Removing seeds from field tomatoes will eliminate excess liquid.
•
Do not toss this salad until just ready to serve.

MAKE AHEAD

Prepare dressing early in the day only if using dried basil. Salad portion can be prepared early in the day.

FROM
ROSE REISMAN'S ENLIGHTENED
HOME COOKING

Four-Tomato Salad

1/2 cup	sun-dried tomatoes	125 mL
2 cups	sliced field tomatoes	500 mL
2 cups	halved red or yellow cherry tomatoes	500 mL
2 cups	quartered plum tomatoes	500 mL
1 cup	sliced red onions	250 mL

Dressing

3 tbsp	olive oil	45 mL
1/4 cup	balsamic vinegar	50 mL
1 1/2 tsp	minced garlic	7 mL
1/2 cup	chopped fresh basil (or 2 tsp [10 mL] dried)	125 mL
1/8 tsp	ground black pepper	0.5 mL

1. Pour boiling water over sun-dried tomatoes. Let rest for 15 minutes until softened. Drain and slice.

2. Place sun-dried tomatoes, field tomatoes, cherry tomatoes, plum tomatoes, red onions and fresh basil in serving bowl or on platter.

3. Whisk together olive oil, balsamic vinegar, garlic and pepper; pour over tomatoes.

Tomato, Potato and Artichoke Salad with Oriental Dressing

1 lb	red potatoes (about 3)	500 g
3	plum tomatoes, seeded	3
1	can (14 oz [398 mL]) artichoke hearts, drained and quartered	1
3/4 cup	chopped red onions	175 mL
1/2 cup	chopped fresh coriander	125 mL
1/3 cup	chopped green onions	75 mL

Dressing

2 tbsp	rice wine vinegar	25 mL
2 tbsp	soya sauce	25 mL
1 tbsp	sesame oil	15 mL
1 tbsp	vegetable oil	15 mL
1 tbsp	honey	15 mL
1 tsp	minced garlic	5 mL
1 tsp	minced ginger root	5 mL

T I P

This salad makes a great side dish or main course.

•

If eaten the next day, this salad will appear wilted but have a more pronounced marinated flavor.

M A K E   A H E A D

Prepare salad and dressing up to 1 day in advance. Best if tossed just before serving.

FROM
ROSE REISMAN'S LIGHT VEGETARIAN COOKING

1. Scrub but do not peel potatoes; cut into 1 1/2 inch (4 cm) pieces and put in a saucepan. Add cold water to cover; bring to a boil, reduce heat to simmer and cook until tender, about 15 minutes. Rinse under cold water and drain.

2. Cut tomatoes into 1 1/2 inch (4 cm) pieces. In a serving bowl, combine potatoes, tomatoes, artichokes, red onions, coriander and green onions.

3. Make the dressing: In a small bowl, whisk together vinegar, soya sauce, sesame oil, vegetable oil, honey, garlic and ginger. Just before serving, pour over salad; toss to coat.

Serves 8 to 10

TIP

Use 3/4 cup (175 mL) store-bought pesto instead of making your own. Keep in mind that calories and fat will be higher.

•

If basil is unavailable, try spinach or parsley leaves.

•

Roasted corn kernels (1 cob) make a delicious replacement for canned kernels. Broil or barbecue corn for 15 minutes or until charred.

MAKE AHEAD

Prepare potatoes, pesto and vegetables up to a day ahead. Toss before serving.

•

Tastes great the next day.

FROM
ROSE REISMAN'S ENLIGHTENED HOME COOKING

Pesto Potato Salad

2 lbs	scrubbed whole red potatoes with skins on	1 kg

Pesto

1 1/4 cups	packed fresh basil leaves	300 mL
3 tbsp	olive oil	45 mL
2 tbsp	toasted pine nuts	25 mL
2 tbsp	grated Parmesan cheese	25 mL
1 tsp	minced garlic	5 mL
1/4 tsp	salt	1 mL
1/4 cup	chicken stock *or* water	50 mL
1 cup	halved snow peas	250 mL
3/4 cup	chopped red onions	175 mL
3/4 cup	chopped red peppers	175 mL
3/4 cup	chopped green peppers	175 mL
1/2 cup	corn kernels	125 mL
2	medium green onions, chopped	2
2 tbsp	toasted pine nuts	25 mL
2 tbsp	lemon juice	25 mL

1. Put potatoes in saucepan with cold water to cover; bring to a boil and cook for 20 to 25 minutes, or until easily pierced with a sharp knife. Drain and set aside.

2. Meanwhile, put basil, olive oil, pine nuts, Parmesan, garlic and salt in food processor; process until finely chopped. With the processor running, gradually add stock through the feed tube; process until smooth.

3. In saucepan of boiling water or microwave, blanch snow peas for 1 or 2 minutes, or until tender-crisp; refresh in cold water and drain. Place in large serving bowl, along with pesto, red onions, red and green peppers, corn, green onions, pine nuts and lemon juice. When potatoes are cool enough to handle, cut into wedges and add to serving bowl; toss well to combine.

Serves 4 to 6

TIP

Make this in summer when tomatoes and basil are at their peak.

FROM
THE ROBERT ROSE
BOOK OF CLASSIC
PASTA

Linguine Salad with Brie Cheese and Tomatoes

1 lb	tomatoes, diced	500 g
8 oz	Brie or Camembert cheese, diced	250 g
1 cup	olive oil	250 mL
1/2 cup	chopped fresh basil (or 1 tbsp [15 mL] dried)	125 mL
1/2 cup	thinly sliced sweet onions (Vidalia, Bermuda or Spanish)	125 mL
1/4 cup	grated Parmesan cheese	50 mL
2 tsp	minced garlic	10 mL
1 lb	linguine	500 g

1. In a large bowl stir together tomatoes, Brie, olive oil, basil, onion, Parmesan and garlic; set aside.

2. In a large pot of boiling salted water, cook linguine 8 to 10 minutes or until *al dente*; drain. Toss with tomato mixture. Chill 1 to 2 hours before serving.

Chilled Penne Tomato Salad

Serves 4

TIP

Make this in summer when tomatoes, basil and peppers are at their peak.

1 lb	tomatoes, diced	500 g
1/2 cup	chopped fresh basil (or 1 tbsp [15 mL] dried)	125 mL
1/2 cup	olive oil	125 mL
1	yellow pepper, thinly sliced	1
2	cloves garlic, crushed	2
12 oz	penne	375 g
	Salt and pepper to taste	

1. In a large bowl, stir together tomatoes, basil, olive oil, pepper strips and garlic.

2. In a large pot of boiling salted water, cook penne 8 to 10 minutes or until *al dente*; drain. Toss with tomato mixture. Season to taste with salt and pepper. Chill 1 hour before serving.

Serves 4

Pea tops are the shoots of snow pea plants. They're now available almost year round in Asian markets. They are tasty in salads and have a subtle, nutty flavor when cooked. However, they are quite perishable and won't last much longer than a couple of days in your refrigerator.

FROM
NEW WORLD CHINESE COOKING BY BILL JONES & STEPHEN WONG

Pea Tops with Pancetta and Tofu

1	3-inch (7.5 cm) square medium tofu	1
2 tbsp	vegetable oil, divided	25 mL
	Salt and pepper to taste	
1 tsp	sesame oil	5 mL
2	slices pancetta *or* prosciutto, finely chopped	2
2 tsp	minced garlic	10 mL
8 oz	pea tops *or* arugula	250 g
2 tbsp	chicken stock *or* vegetable stock	25 mL

1. Slice tofu into pieces 1/2 inch (1 cm) thick by 1 1/2 inches (3.5 cm) square.

2. In a nonstick skillet, heat 1 tbsp (15 mL) oil over medium-high heat for 30 seconds. Add tofu and season lightly with salt, pepper and sesame oil; fry until golden, about 1 minute per side. Remove from skillet; arrange on a platter and keep warm.

3. Add remaining oil to skillet; heat for 30 seconds. Add pancetta and garlic; fry briefly until fragrant, about 20 to 30 seconds. Add pea tops and stock; stir-fry until pea tops are just wilted. Arrange evenly over tofu and serve.

To toast almonds, heat a dry heavy skillet over medium heat for 30 seconds. Add almonds and cook until they begin to turn golden, about 2 minutes. Immediately remove from heat, as they'll continue cooking until they cool.

FROM
NEW WORLD
NOODLES BY BILL JONES &
STEPHEN WONG

Rice Noodle Salad with Sugar Snap Peas, Sweet Peppers and Almonds with Nuoc Cham

8 oz	medium vermicelli (rice stick noodles) *or* dried fettuccine	250 g
2/3 cup	NUOC CHAM (see recipe, page 27)	150 mL
1 tbsp	butter	15 mL
1 tbsp	olive oil	15 mL
3 cups	trimmed sugar snap or snow peas	750 mL
2 tsp	minced garlic	10 mL
2 tbsp	vegetable or chicken stock	25 mL
1 cup	thinly sliced red bell peppers	250 mL
1 cup	thinly sliced yellow bell peppers	250 mL
1/2 cup	toasted sliced almonds	125 mL
1/4 cup	cilantro leaves	50 mL
	Coarsely ground black pepper, to taste	

1. In a heatproof bowl or pot, cover noodles with boiling water and soak for 5 minutes. (If using pasta, prepare according to package directions.) Drain, toss with 1/3 cup (75 mL) of the NUOC CHAM and let cool to room temperature.

2. In a nonstick pan, heat butter and oil over medium-high heat until just smoking. Add peas and stir-fry until well-coated, about 30 seconds. Add garlic and stock. Cover and cook until peas are tender-crisp, about 1 minute. Add peppers and stir-fry until warmed through and liquid is absorbed, about 1 minute. Remove from heat. Add remaining NUOC CHAM and mix well.

3. In a large salad bowl, combine noodles, vegetables, almonds and cilantro; toss. Sprinkle with black pepper to taste and serve.

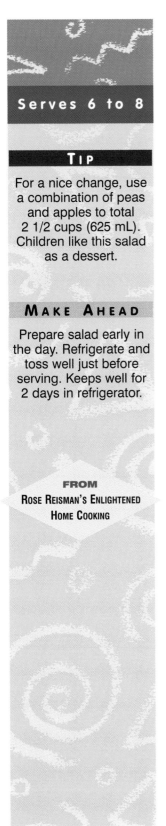

Serves 6 to 8

TIP

For a nice change, use a combination of peas and apples to total 2 1/2 cups (625 mL). Children like this salad as a dessert.

MAKE AHEAD

Prepare salad early in the day. Refrigerate and toss well just before serving. Keeps well for 2 days in refrigerator.

FROM
ROSE REISMAN'S ENLIGHTENED HOME COOKING

Sweet Cinnamon Waldorf Salad

2 1/2 cups	diced apples	625 mL
3/4 cup	diced celery	175 mL
1 cup	red or green seedless grapes, quartered	250 mL
1 cup	chopped red or green peppers	250 mL
1/3 cup	raisins	75 mL
1/2 cup	canned mandarin oranges, drained	125 mL
2 tbsp	finely chopped pecans	25 mL

Dressing

1/4 cup	light mayonnaise	50 mL
1/4 cup	light (1%) sour cream	50 mL
2 tbsp	honey	25 mL
1 tbsp	lemon juice	15 mL
1/2 tsp	cinnamon	2 mL

1. In a serving bowl, combine apples, celery, grapes, sweet peppers, raisins, mandarin oranges and pecans.

2. In small bowl, combine mayonnaise, sour cream, honey, lemon juice and cinnamon; mix thoroughly. Pour over salad and toss.

Grilled Vegetable Salad

1	medium zucchini	1
1	medium sweet red pepper	1
Half	large red onion	Half
12	small mushrooms	12
3 cups	mixed lettuce leaves (Boston, romaine, radicchio)	750 mL

Dressing

2 tbsp	lemon juice	25 mL
2 tbsp	water	25 mL
1 tbsp	brown sugar	15 mL
4 tsp	balsamic vinegar	20 mL
1 tsp	crushed garlic	5 mL
2 tbsp	olive oil	25 mL
	Salt and pepper	

1. Cut zucchini, red pepper and onion into 2-inch (5 cm) chunks. Alternately thread along with mushrooms onto barbecue skewers.

2. Dressing: In small bowl, combine lemon juice, water, sugar, vinegar and garlic; gradually whisk in oil. Season with salt and pepper to taste. Pour into dish large enough to hold skewers.

3. Add skewers to dressing; marinate for 20 minutes, turning often.

4. Grill vegetables until tender, basting with dressing and rotating often, approximately 15 minutes.

5. Remove vegetables from skewers and place on lettuce-lined serving platter. Pour any remaining dressing over vegetables.

Yam and Pecan Salad

Serves 4 to 6

This is a spectacular salad that will gain new fans for the sweet smoothness of the nutritious but neglected yam. The pecans are a slight extravagance (both financial and caloric), but they add crunch and significant luxury. The colorful concoction works as a lively appetizer, as well as one course of a celebratory, slightly exotic buffet.

FROM
THE NEW VEGETARIAN
GOURMET BY BYRON
AYANOGLU

PREHEAT OVEN TO 450° F (230° C)
BAKING DISH GREASED WITH 1 TBSP (15 ML) VEGETABLE OIL

1 lb	yams, unpeeled but well scrubbed	500 g
Half	red bell pepper, cut into thick strips	Half
1/4 cup	vegetable oil	50 mL
1 tsp	mustard seeds	5 mL
Pinch	cayenne	Pinch
Pinch	cinnamon	Pinch
Pinch	ground cumin	Pinch
1/3 cup	pecan halves	75 mL
3 tbsp	lime juice	45 mL
1 tsp	sesame oil	5 mL
1/2 tsp	salt	2 mL
1/2 cup	thinly slivered red onions	125 mL
	Few sprigs fresh coriander, chopped	

1. In a large saucepan cover yams with plenty of water and bring to a boil. Cook for 10 minutes, then drain. Cut yams into rounds 1/2 inch (1 cm) thick.

2. In prepared baking dish, arrange the sliced yams and red pepper strips in a single layer. Bake in the preheated oven for 12 to 15 minutes, until the yams are easily pierced with a fork.

3. Meanwhile, in a frying pan, heat the oil over medium heat for 1 minute. Add mustard seeds, cayenne, cinnamon and cumin, and stir-fry for 2 minutes, or until spices begin to pop. Add the pecans; stir-fry for 2 minutes until the nuts have browned a little on both sides (don't burn them). Remove from heat and reserve spices in pan.

4. Remove yams and red peppers from the oven. Using a spatula, carefully transfer them onto a serving plate, making a single layer.

5. Drizzle lime juice and sesame oil over the yams and sprinkle with salt. Scatter slivers of red onion on top. Using a spoon and a rubber spatula, scrape contents of the frying pan (pecans, oil and spices) evenly over the yams. Let salad rest for 10 to 15 minutes, then garnish with the chopped coriander and serve.

Serves 4 to 6

TIP

This recipe can be pre-pared using all wild rice or all white rice.

•

Great salad for brunch or picnic. Sits well for hours.

MAKE AHEAD

Prepare up to a day ahead. Keep refrigerated and stir well before serving.

FROM
ROSE REISMAN'S ENLIGHTENED HOME COOKING

Polynesian Wild Rice Salad

2 cups	chicken stock	500 mL
1/2 cup	white rice	125 mL
1/2 cup	wild rice	125 mL
1 cup	halved snow peas	250 mL
1 cup	chopped red peppers	250 mL
3/4 cup	chopped celery	175 mL
2/3 cup	sliced water chestnuts	150 mL
1/2 cup	canned mandarin oranges, drained	125 mL
2	medium green onions, chopped	2

Dressing

2 tsp	orange juice concentrate, thawed	10 mL
2 tsp	honey	10 mL
1 tsp	soya sauce	5 mL
1 tsp	vegetable oil	5 mL
1/2 tsp	sesame oil	2 mL
1/2 tsp	lemon juice	2 mL
1/2 tsp	minced garlic	2 mL
1/4 tsp	minced ginger root	1 mL

1. Bring stock to boil in medium saucepan; add wild rice and white rice. Cover, reduce heat to medium low and simmer for 15 to 20 minutes, or until rice is tender and liquid is absorbed. Rinse with cold water. Put rice in serving bowl.

2. In a saucepan of boiling water or microwave, blanch snow peas for 1 or 2 minutes or until tender-crisp; refresh in cold water and drain. Add to serving bowl along with red peppers, celery, water chestnuts, mandarin oranges and green onions; toss well.

3. In small bowl, whisk together orange juice concentrate, honey, soya sauce, vegetable oil, sesame oil, lemon juice, garlic and ginger; pour over salad and toss well.

Index

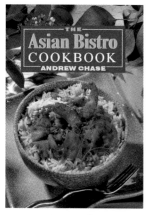

More of your favorite recipes

Just about everyone loves pasta. After all, there are few types of food that can be prepared in so many interesting ways. And that's what you'll discover in this book — over 50 recipes that range from classic comfort foods such as macaroni and cheese to more exotic Asian-inspired noodle dishes.   **ISBN 1-896503-74-8**

Here's a book for all the people who love desserts, but worry about all the fat and calories. Imagine being able to indulge, guilt-free, in luscious cheesecakes, pies — even chocolate desserts! Well, now you can. Choose from a variety of after-dinner treats that contain less than 200 calories per serving.   **ISBN 1-896503-72-1**

What can you serve that's guaranteed to please everyone? Chichen, of course! And here you'll find over 50 superb recipes — ranging from comfort foods like Chicken-Vegetable Cobbler to a more sophisticated Chicken Breasts Stuffed with Brie Cheese, Red Pepper and Green Onions. A must for every kitchen.   **ISBN 1-896503-53-5**

Cook along with bestselling author Rose Reisman as she prepares over 50 of her favorite dishes — including soups, burgers, chili and cheesecakes. Each section features helpful, step-by-step pictures that demonstrate a particular technique. Over 100 color images in all.
ISBN 1-896503-28-4